Poet-Trees by The Jordan River

Published by Spines
ISBN: 979-8-89691-070-1

Poet-Trees by The Jordan River

Tresha Dorce

My Dear Daddy God,

You have graced me with this gift and I am giving it back to You. Thank You for every church family, family member, friend and professor who encouraged me through my poetry writing journey. May each word that You have so richly bestowed upon my spirit and onto every page, bless the heart of every reader. From the title to the very last word within this book, let Your name be glorified.

Everlasting love,

Your baby girl

Introduction

Transition relentlessly strikes the
    Jordan River,
compassionately consuming tears of persistence
courageously caressing faith filled expectation,
through Heaven's gentle hands
graced by redemptive power.
Obedience, anticipation harmonize
    and
stride into
earth's road to
eternal promises
bearing up weariness
of former enemies.
Ages
......passing
    forward, with lips inspired by Love's
fiery gaze of instructions to endlessly
thrust into the miraculous.

A

POETIC

HARMONY

Calling YOU DADDY GOD

Deeper than all oceans deep,
wider than every valley wide
filling every empty space inside,
my world is all right,
when I call YOU, Sweet Dearest DADDY GOD.

Though unseen wounds softly speak, causing pain
beneath YOUR precious palm such afflictions dwell in
vain.
DADDY GOD, thank YOU for showing me the gravity of
YOUR work
never will I cease to learn.

On YOUR index finger I rest,
at times unable to stand the
test.
With more power than I will never own
YOU encourage me to stretch.

YOU are King and YOU call me Princess
bowing down I receive, sheltered in YOUR glory.
I am splendidly graced; YOU own my destiny.
Daily triumphant, with YOUR genes locked in me.

Prophetically Supreme Father of Nations

Loving is your golden heart, for countless sheep across
nations
who drink from a Divinely orchestrated stream
birthed from a heavenly agreement
established upon your spirit
passionately yielding
yes, to Daddy God,
a glorious place of
sacred, secret, sacrifices
with Heaven
descending to embrace
the fruit of your lips.
Angels surround the parameters of your dwelling place
saturated by Daddy God's passionate glory,
drenched in your compassionate Prophetic intercession
of love, for the bride of Christ.
Heaven's aroma embodies your every move
and embraces your obedience.
Your children look to you
instructed by the sweet loving cadence
of your heartbeat for Daddy God's will
and treasures veiled in Heaven's Chamber.
Yes, your little children look to you
empowered
by the destruction you strike

towards darkness
by sharp two-edged substances
protruding from Daddy God's Mind
occupying every fragment of your being
Alleluia!
Across the globe your children are
delivered, healed and restored by
your presence soaked
in Daddy God's oil
flowing from you
to us and
with you before us
we, as an army cleave to your Prophetic footsteps
and stand to sing
Forever Victorious!

Celestially Gracious Mother of Nations

Graciously and in peace you stride
and guide
your children beyond
oceans, rivers, cities, towns, valleys and continents
by your soothing smile of
motherly embrace
we are captivated
and freely gravitate
resting in
the palm of your nurturing words of fire
powerfully extracted from
Daddy God's genetic roots
from the depth of your love courage, strength and
wisdom
many fruits arise
upholding the vision
embedded in
our father's prophetic stride.
Heaven's smile surrounds your
victorious touch
that ever so richly
imparts healing upon
broken souls, hearts, lives
are changed.
Within Daddy God's Throne room

your spirit yields
as your worship caresses His heart
gloriously,
your smile of praise
to our Heavenly Father
releases
daggers destroying darkness
in the midst of heavy obstacles
your presence gracefully dispatches
peace, upon the hearts of your children
empowering them
to relentlessly
March in Victory!

Heaven's Spoken Seed

This seed purposed destiny
lies in wait
in secret space
counts to 9 until...
Release.
From Heavens
Breath
this seed incepts.
Daddy God's novel,
Written before time knew
Time......
From every paragraph to every phrase
and every chapter to every page
painted on my Father's canvass
sculpted by His cautious stroke
a soft Divine Kiss
Speaks this seed into shape.
This seed, that seed,
is me!

Stepping

A single touch of Divine bloom and beauty

travels through my short

growing

existence, and

my mind gradually

marring tangibility

consumes rapidly

the world around me.

The words: home and mommy. Wait!

Mommy so sweet to me.

mY mOmmY

That smile, that laugh, that blissful swag
pepper salt sassy hair tied up in a silk purple rag,
high cheek bones
pretty thin catty eyes
love the way you sit and rise
high pitched smiles and low-pitched frowns
slow, swift sashay
from the kitchen to the lounge
from the lounge to the kitchen
checkin' on cookin' beans, rice and chicken
shoulder sagging down of off life's blues
still in joyful mood
you conquer and move
feeding family
in spirit and in tummy.
Out in the breeze
we sing "Just a closer walk with thee"
spring time joins
growing flowers and leaves.
Defining Moments, writes Jacqueline Thomas,
the book we watch the television we read
let's sit and have a glass of iced tea.

Brother and Me

Down to earth and cool
from breezing morning strolls '
to school, where we
learn rules
and follow molecules
from the classroom to the
dining room
dinner ready!
Swims between
our teeth to our belly,
high fiving we chat
fist bumping we talk.
In the midst of unspoken
dialogue caressing every thought,
concealed in frowns that smile.
In a room our loving retaliation
punches and shouts.
Even when our hugs sting,
our love goes hard.

F-A-I-T-H

From a warrior sequestered
resting at infancy's core
with many questions in the midst
faith overcomes, masked in flesh
and glorious intricacy
Faith so beautiful
delicate in countless facets
yet irresistibly
filled with might
a warrior vigorously
resting in her.
Faith silently
kicks through storms of doubt
Faith………..grows.
Though challenged……reaches the…
                        other side in
a powerfully unseen world
small, seemingly powerless,
Faith shoves stormy winds out of sight
breaking walls with
Godly might and……
now faith is amongst us.
Yes, she is and pleasantly
releasing hopes precious aroma.

Sparking
laughter, love , joy, peace, purpose and revival.

Sweet Sisterhood Jewels

My sisters
sweet sisters I cherish your love.
Through childhood's charm a third grade bond formed a
forever..... high pitched hello and
low pitched
goodbye, even when we cry,
Best Friend Holy Spirit's Smile hides the sorrows of life.
Harmony sashays between us,
undying laughs and smirks
wise jokes told,
strength and gladness
in the field
of winning souls
sisters help
spiritual and academic growth,
from diapers to sharpeners and
sharpeners to 20-paged papers
we graduate and life sings to the steps
of our gracious stilettos.
Joyously shouting in church and dashing to work,
unstoppable dreams....... victorious,
we stick together for life, indeed.

Cousins Connection

East 96th street celebrates our
union, barbeque dancing balloons
firefly catchin' days.
Childhood imagination
containing money hoping
   out of
leaves to five cent peanut chews wrappers
prancing
   along the sidewalk of destiny.
Our hearts combined through ups
and downs.
Harmoniously drenched by
tears, wide distance fades,
climbing years yet
ageless unity.
Two kisses away
across the states
sweet cousins stay
in education's canopy
very little time to celebrate
but strong bond still remains.

Man of Godly Compassion

Within each fragment of your being

Daddy God's, Breathing Word resides

and flourishes, eradicating wickedness.

Humility embraces your smile,

integrity captivates your stride.

Looking up into your eyes,

the church sees long fruitful life.

You complement the

Heartbeat of Christ,

from your womb heavenly words flow

into thirsty souls,

through salvations intro,

Heavenly word filled disciples grow,

with you presiding and

Daddy God shining,

His Eternal smile upon You.

Woman of Great Faith

With noble kingdom beauty

you stand on heavenly words

so deeply rooted

in you.

Embedded in your

prestigious steps

faith and love

ever true.

Wisdom

drips elegantly

from the crown

of your head

saturating your surrounding.

Your anointing

graciously resounding

penetrates every wounded soul

From brokenness,

people grow.

Your vision forever embracing

Daddy God's mind

in His word you abide.

With each long stride

specks of darkness shrivel

Beneath your feet.

At your illustrious entrance

people gaze,

while Divinity's loving grace

never ceases to enfold

the incredible You.

Man of Great Wisdom

Wisdom, wrapped in the

womb of your speech,

lends a relentless thrust

into the victorious street

of life's testing journey.

In silence, your wisdom leads,

granting clarity in mystery.

Your sons and daughters live

triumphantly, shooting wisdom

in the heart of adversity.

With tender authority you speak

and your children discover keys

unlocking victory and liberty

to dream big and succeed,

upholding integrity.

Kingdom Lady: Vessel of Greatness

Beautiful sweet fragrance caramel sexy glow
                    sassy shiny black locks
                        great big sparkly eyes
tickle me funny bones jokes on the side
             pretty smile touching cute baby doll lips
tall prestigious fascination
          soft and firm to the touch

Heavenly guided fingers capturing prosperous elegance

Divine DNA filled words
          Target spiritual wounds

          Restoration
          anew.

That is all I wonder,
                thinking of You!

Forever, a Glorious Legacy

Upon infancy's steps your tears vigorously, climbed

drenching Daddy Gods ears and with a single thrust

toward a sweet selfless maternal vessel

Divine activation of hidden treasures danced

within you and

your feet soaked in fiery beauty stretched across

global bridges firmly embellished with

Daddy God's Voice

of instructions

rooted and pacing at the very core of your hearts

passion and

compassion from the

     center

of your soul

    poured out

in the midst of dry places where healing, deliverance and
miracles

no longer constrained, exhale.

From the ministry's secret chamber, angelic midwives

consistently propel

the steps of devout vessels

to glean upon the threshing floor of the vision

embedded in your heart: Forever a Glorious Legacy.

A legacy continuously unleashing hidden treasures
found in

Daddy God's image.

In a glorious glistening and golden

atmosphere

you are embraced by royalty's excellence

and with grace

your reward penetrates, the desires

of so many calling you Pa Pa

passionately aspire

to imitate your gracious and noble race.

Legendary Race

Noble race reigns with praise
at the heart of
your legacy, where your love and
treasured rib overflowing with courage strength
love, faith, grace and beauty
yes Ma Ma to so many
swaddles the heart of your legacy
at the core of her loving embrace.
Dedication enfolding her steps
while Sons and daughters grow
from the garden of heavens bosoms
where Ma Ma's prayers are
engraved and
sustained
to nurture legacy's offspring ever moving
and plowing the ground for
scattered souls
to forever thrive
in oneness
and shine
with Gospel's undying glow.

Brotherhood Bravery

Dignified defense over

wife, children,

mother, sister, auntie and

grandmother,

brothers, your chest puffed,

shoulders squared, roar

throughout the platform of

existing aggression, even in

High-pitched noiseless sensitivity,

you choke the sting of adversity

with hands used to swaddle your baby.

Brothers, you uphold humility,

facing flying fiery darts, assertively.

Your tears sing courageously

and your laugh weakens the very

obstacles rushing toward your home.

Uncles and Aunties

Uncles and Aunties your words

empower.

A touch of faith

mixed with the warmth

of wise counsel,

trickles to the root of

my soul's intellect.

Aunties,

every ingredient

of love, joy and hope

protrude from your pot of

hospitality

rendering

fragrance of

comfort.

The nostrils of your loved ones,

are satiated and

from your fingertips

      steam

Divine sustenance

to treat ponderous spirits

and wailing hearts.

You fasten the ropes

preserving union amongst

every heartbeat.

Uncles, your husky speech leaves

a lasting…..indentation

of sharp-witted beauty in

present souls and generations to

come. Wisdom glides through

every stride you take.

With outstretched biceps

you fortify gracefully.

Your pride smiles with humility

and your years embrace integrity.

Grandparents

Every one of your seeds are captured and secured.

Grandparents

Your sagacious hands confidently bear the weight of
generations
to come,
circumspectly your eyes penetrate the destiny of each
progeny………………….and faithfully diligent fingers
fabricate provision
substance creatively arising
from fragments of laughter, pain, joy and brokenness
gather and pour upon parched naïve soul.

Grandparents

Your legacy continuously breaths through
hearts, minds and lips of
your offspring,
sharp-witted words protruding from
your spirit fortifies the steps of those
who follow
Footprint you leave and
harvest you reap.

Grandparents

Even in the chamber of mortal [silence]
your existence remains,
rooted in the pool of multicolored traits
arising on the surface of every seed
with heartfelt gratitude we advance and freely flow
through the streams of your sweat, tears and blood.

Heavens Gift on Resurrection Sunday

Heavens precious bundle of incredibility

conserved with delightful intricacy

before earth comprehending can see

on Resurrection Sunday.

Daddy Gods Beauty revealing

a king sheltered in an infant

temporarily.

A mighty warrior

upholding victoriously

the banner of Blood-stained Divinity,

an anointed leader rebelling righteously

against final wickedly tainted times. Daddy Gods

elected ruler instructing a holy assembly into

everlasting.

A precious baby sent from Heaven to earth,

for such a time as, Resurrection Sunday!

Heaven's Victorious Ambassadors

Triumphantly, even through trials

we march

vigilantly, with Prophetic guidance

carved on the staff of our Moses.

A strategic stance reflecting Divine logos and

rhema enfolds our feet

planted on our undefeatable Altar,

Prophetically guarded by fruits

strongly sprouting from the roots, of our

Parents' prayers, praise, worship and love,

gracefully, spreading across the globe.

With our vision glued to the prize

drenched in Jesus' blood for all

we arise

stronger

moving forward in Victory.

Calvary

Marveling we gaze up at the
tree of intimacy
covered in redeeming blood reaching
down to secure Heavens kiss in our souls.
Saturated in Love's aroma
our praise penetrates walls
to break
in the midst of Worship's bridge
to Love's Heart:
Chamber of Mystery.
We grow gradually into
Loves head, heart, hands and feet
propelling foreign babes to gravitate.
A harmonious army gathered
with our youth trained to
lead with royal's trace
we sing, worship and praise
prevailing over
Crucifixion's pain
forever to be raised in LOVE.

Evangelical Heart

Captured by LOVE

my childlike soul freely

enfolds, your hands

suppressed by Jesus'

sweet embrace

drenched in saving Blood

proceeding with Grace

our heartbeat celebrates

Daddy Gods Love

for my simple footsteps

to listen

taking heed to

dance into the tabernacle

marking

Salvation's foundation.

Gradually I spring higher

at the beautiful taste of Daddy God's

seed encapsulating my Destiny

so gracefully. My steps

mount

my Spiritual Journey

gratefully bows

as worship's aroma

ascends into Heavens gates

where angels smile shine

and

Daddy Gods hands forever

caress your ever so sweet

Evangelical heart.

Salvation's Foundation

In the tabernacle
upholding salvations womb
I stand surrounded by scriptures
abundantly floating
to penetrate the pores
of my
untrained
hungry
armor consuming
victory to bring
inescapable darts of darkness
down to shame.
My spirit growing
cleaves to Loves gracious feet
and elevates upon
the pages
of Daddy Gods comforting
Breath.
Fourteen encircles the phase
of encountering the depth of Loves
Heart drenched in redeeming blood
so intimately enfolded forever
crucified
I rise with Love.

Journey With Daddy God:

Fighting

into

the

Treasure

Chess

It all began

Angel's voices, hymns so sweet

just a bus roll down the street

I was fifteen

when eye shifting revelation,

of Divine rest

delivered,

a spirit stroking breath,

brought on a smile

continuing throughout

millions of blocks

and hundreds of miles,

street pictures motion

in windows view,

following smooth, rolling, cadence

of the bus.

Unforgettable. Fear

of losing. Such pearly white

misty canine digging through

dark chocolate covered cream and cherries.

Unexplainable. Faith

to be saturated, blinded

but knowing the land of

milk and honey.

On our mid-section

switching earth,

everything that was,

everything that is

and everything to come.

But what is to come?

In moments singing pleasant

Now for me.

Now for me

On my knees.
My spirit liberally receives,
substance to encapsulate
fragments of my precious coming Groom
who once, and for all,
bled LOVE from His Heavenly root.
Prostrate upon this cushioned,
golden platform
I lay. The veil, embraces us.
With pomegranate covered
fragrance,
my hair sweetly damped,
rest at His unblemished guiding feet.
An unspoken transaction graciously groans
delightfully………………..reaching, SHARP!
Moans, at the throne room.
His heaviness seeps through
my strength depleted,
I…… sleep.

I Sleep...........

I.........Sleep.

Ahhhhhhhhhh.

Daddy God I am so in love with You

let Your hug swallow me

till no more of,

me becoming

about You and,

only all of You.

Only , All Of You.

But   Something

I don't know what.

Something sneaking from a

pitfall of a musty black womb.

What?

No, it can't be.

Please No!

please just let it be,

forever Big Brother Jesus and me and

angels on the bus, sound sings and

Sweet Best Friend Holy Spirit,

while,

Daddy God's touch rings

vibrations through my

sleeping spirit.

But something screams

scratching blood from

my innermost being

disturbing to me

something dragging me to

nearly sink

weeping my consistent why,

I try

to run and [hide]

but something rides

and now I see,

Something has

             a name, a face

                 something has a season

                 and place

engulfing pain seek I to erase. But

peace helplessly drowns through

tears….overflowing…..

I told you

I see teeth gnashing something,

digging into innocence's past

remaining dormant in

the elastically firmed, cushioned

wrapper of life

evidence calls

brain chewing something

from below

eye ball plucking,

squeezing to pus,

heart clutching

something's

DOWN   ON

THE

                        OTHER SIDE!!!!!!!!!!!!!!

The Unseen

On the bus, dark attack
dances before me
but...
Angels send fiery
darts to defend
my peace.
Sight forbidding muddy beings
blow trashy flames.
Angles shift in
battle facing me on their
mission,
they say: "We got your back."
On the rolling bus
I seek to speak the unseen
but the language of a
wacko is what some see.
I sweat sorrow to push
through sleepless
nights shoving me awake
in between the clock's finger's,
at the Hiltons.
I scream
blindness, walks into the eyes of my
loved ones
helplessly,

missing the boisterous battle
raging before me.
I call to Daddy God and
He tells me: "The battle is over
Baby girl,
they were after
My Substance."
I smile at His priceless
Dialect of assurance,
to Him I rejoice
infused with victory
The Angels join me
I am free
Flapping through a breeze
Of ease
The Angles,
My Angels
Go up, up
they go UP.

UP in Eternity

The Angels continue
in celebration with
Daddy God, and
Big Brother Jesus.
Families breathing thousands
upon thousands of ages
joins hands with the
new members who await
future families.
Sweet house of Eternity
cupping, silver, gold and pearls
dancing songs, singing twirls.
The mansions, both big and small
running golden streets
HOLY is the music of
four creatures
and constant to the
rhythm is the worship
of twenty-four elders.
No lines, no boundaries,
all in all, adventures.
Crystal multicolored robes
swinging over bronze and emerald.
unable to travel

ever in full
for eternity in pace
wraps eternity in space.

Experiences

Reflections

Restoration

Childhood Container
moving on

83 STREET
the block of the year
from ten to twenty five
eye blinking ages swung by

back in the days
Issac Bildersee park
Mid Education 68
    tag playing
   basketball scoring
      arms in the air
  shorts and jersey's
     say heyyyyy!

     Bike Riding
         down the ally
   smiling sun shines,
      a truck load of fun
     moving
    Upstairs as life seasons

        shift into
      God's keepsake

spoken years before
at the thirsty, lip chapping,
weeping gut wilderness.

   But in the new
      Still walking
     pass Ralph Avenue
      South Shore High School
      conquers
      marking one block's spot

        Bildersee the same
  never forgetting former days,
  sixth grade teachers so sweet.
  At the bodega after three
  the boys and girls meet
  chip chewin',
 drink gulpin'
  bubble gum poppin'
 days running
back to beacon after school
mind building platform
     Sheepshead Bay High school
      transition
      abruptly
   four years
   appear at Walt Whitman Hall
   caps and gowns, band playing moment.
   Picture capturing smiles, laughs

and cry's
friends will be missed.

Now and again form
the academic battlefield to
the academic red carpet
dazzling burgundy
caps and gowns
enfolding
pencils, papers and pens soaring to
Higher

Heights

approaching seasons awaits
new

life begins!

Brooklyn College Experience

A single hop
protrudes from a few of
life's Annual, Expedient, Vapor
and initiates an unfamiliar
season, that creeps into, the,
usual aspect of my being.
The taste of familiar, shrinks
upon my tongue, yet my
feet frowns at the unknown.
Nevertheless, time stretches forth
his hands and embraces my uncertainty,
Driving me into a series of pages
secured in Daddy Gods novel of me.
From a succession of heavy curricular syllabi to,
Lipke's lab of science spectacle,
my Academic Walk of Victory
presents itself after sweating many
exams and papers and in a
flash,
my years sashay unpredictably,
in the same setting,
finals short portion meets
beginnings maturity.

Just Trippin'

On a Sunny afternoon
I walk way down Ralph Avenue
dashing to cross the street,
Kingdom sistah girl stops me for a greet
we say hi, kiss ya, miss ya, huggin' seconds we split

Sweating out a starting stroll,
I stopped at Telco,
just for a quick stare
with a quick shift I head downstairs

and held a plastic bin up to Ms. Cashier
from my wallet I pay the due
and swiftly out the door I flew
slowing down to catch my breath
I saw no need to rush
with an 1 hour and 30 minutes left
enough time to hit more dust
before ma ma and I catch the bus
I walk to Walbaum…Yay! Wheat Thins on sale
four boxes I bought and made my way to the trail.
I met ma ma at the bus stop
on the bus we sat,
to move until our finger says stop.

Stick-It –Forgetfulness

Though carved in my mind
It
touches me none.
It
reappearing
It
reaches for
my healing heart
It
I punch
It
I kick
down to sensitivity
It
once imposed on me,
seeking to tear
my precious beating blood
It remaining
but to me
It
fading
I say goodbye but,
It,
says,
HELL-OOOO.

Pain........ Remembering to Forget

The boldness that speaks through you,

stands quietly yet everyone hears it.

Your words embrace the lips of your loved ones

enabling their feet to shy away from needless failure.

Oh, Mother of many, my ears hearing are unable to listen.

Sitting at the temple, my mind…refusing to hold

the truth of such meeting.

Powerless am I to watch the

ground swallow you…...refusing to agree

but must accept. I must leave the moment short returning
to life.

Living. Waking from bed my, eyes

capture emptiness creeping through my heart.

Oh, what a beautiful stone with your name neatly
engraved,

but with nature carelessly staring back at me,

I……….refusing to believe

that once upon a time it surrounded you.

Father's Void

Father……..emptiness stares back,

at question marks.

Little girl me looks up and

down at confusion filled hurt

locked in over 6 feet of

existence…. existed hands

swelled up by agony

stabbed purity in me.

Regretfully wounds

choke purity in me

from roaring infant

to weeping lion,

vindictively instant,

over six feet of

confusion filled hurt

conceal shameful dirt,

anticipating silence.

But purity victoriously

scarred speaks in me

growing more victorious

than scarred, captured by

Heaven's Paternal Vault.

Daddy God's Hands swiftly

Rescues, purity in me

from confusion filled hurt's

heavy shadow. Traveling

through everlasting WORD

purity grows

in me, comforted

by Grace's daily caress.

Until purity in me no longer stressed,

but free.

I am free!!!

Dream Big Again

To dream big again
and fly through the
shine and shade of
our tomorrow
forgetting yesterdays sorrow
we rest upon a
sweet rolling rainbow
singing to the King of Kings
who brings hope overflowing
to dream big again.
Though our wounds
………..Cry………..
Faith and courage arise
unraveling a landscape
for our dreams to
step out and dance
in spite of
yesterday's painful mud pit
endurance whispered through
stormy winds
empowering our dreams to
withstand temporary incarceration.
Let us stretch our vision beyond
man's reach

for prosperous future calls
For us to dream big again

Pleading Patience

The strolling years passed
in their stillness.
A million more times have I waited
to see beauty, wrapped
in hand clutching anticipation
once promised.
Gazing through
Daddy God's Literary Splendor
protagonist's endurance
finds strength in
reader's curiosity
become one and
tarry…………until the end.
Beyond bright blue skies,
my eyes searching, speaks and
receives Divine understanding
to wait,
in moments unsure of worthwhile motion
embracing faith not just within…..
        promises fulfilled,
but also to see satisfying substance in view of noth-
ingness.

On That Day

On that day,

when I see for

years have I waited,

to see the hidden climbing,

in the womb of my heart,

effortlessly springing ,

it expands toward the surface.

And now my heart,

the sweet chamber of

the unspoken pounding,

over pressure

hopes never to burst,

releasing fragments

captured by unfinished substance.

Substance once seen in its fullness,

when Heavens

open door revealed,

Daddy God's,

Exquisite, Sculptural, Delight,

of what is to come from that door

shutting before my eyes, the door

to my heart.

But still I anticipate the full promise

Of Divine Masterpiece,

relishing in Daddy Gods,

finishing touch,

I embrace the unseen

in His presence,

no longer to be in the

confinement of suspense,

my heart,

oh, precious and faithful container

through divine strength

steadily bearing,

glorious heaviness

believing on that day,

to release and rest.

Today I see that day,

I see the unseen

and rejoice, to

pour out the

sight catching fragrance

locked in

my heart,

upon

Daddy God's feet.

I see the unseen

And adorn its path, with praises

to my King, yes praises

To my KING.

Worship's Path

Entering the castle surrounded by silver and gold,
wrapped in her linen gown a sweet
scent of pomegranate and cherries tra-
ils before the King's throne,
where treasures locked in vessels lie,
one pleasurable dance soon tickles the soles of her feet.
Across the golden platform her movement is carried by
the beat.
The sound of cymbals and drums boisterously folds
both flute and lyres soothing flow.
Great privilege she has in the presence of her King.
Entering the castle she looks at fine gold,
where treasures locked in vessels lie,
one with the vessels, wrapped in Divine majesty.
She enters with delight, behind the veil of purity.
Behind the veil of purity deep within a
        secret
place, her Husband, King and Redeemer awaits.
Beyond her control, through His Holy Wind she floats
to find herself, barefoot saturated with joyous tears.
Breaking her priceless box, the contents drench her hair.

Totally surrendering at His feet
her worship so full, dives deeply
penetrating His Heart.
His Appreciation complementing her joy.
Broken and humble her hair wipes his feet.
Less of her and more of Him.
Her cup once empty now carries more,
moving on, whole and stronger than before.

The Journey of LOVE

Trickling from the heart of
majesty Redemption speaks,
as Divine Seed strides through pearly gates
to penetrate imperfections core.
Upholding a flesh filled door Love runs
through muddy walls to embrace,
His wife
into everlasting life.
LOVE in infancy
exposes splendor of
Royalty's concealment.
In our midst , Love travels
Dwelling in
the cushion of maternity and
shield of Paternity.
However, with a swift blow
of destiny
33 years tilts releasing the flow
of Loves glorious space, upon
sinful ground.
Saving and raising from everlasting death,
Love suffered in mortality's nest,
once and for always, we can be free
Remaining in His rest.

THE PENTOCOST

Fifty days swept pass the calendar.

After our sweet Jesus kissed goodbye,

we watched as the descending sky,

raised him high,

attentively, the clouds embraced our KING,

quickly fading

before our eyes, only to return one day

to say: welcome home my bride.

Fifty days, fifty days fifty days, we tarry

while heavenly wonderment

strolls into our finite minds

revealing, blood punching from flesh,

beaten by Divinity

on a tree,

He presents, our Engagement ring.

Time of His passionate reappearance to us, unknown

yet continuously we flow upon His didactic shadow

until an immediate Fifty days, strikes humanity

as Heavens Fingers, propel Holy Fire,

through incomprehensible speech.

Pointing, some speak mockery

but believe,

believe God's royal clock ticks

His word on earth shall always be seen.

FIFTY DAYS.